BUILDING RESILIENT COMMUNITIES

SOCIAL WORK IN ACTION

DR. MINAKSHI BANSAL

DEDICATION

This work is dedicated to all those who stand at the front lines of community resilience: the social workers, community leaders, educators, and volunteers whose tireless efforts underpin the strength and spirit of their communities. Your unwavering commitment and deep compassion not only inspire hope during challenging times but also forge the path toward a more resilient future for us all. Thank you for your dedication and for reminding us that in the heart of community lies the power of unity and perseverance.

❧

Contents

Prayer — vii

About the Author — ix

Preface — xiii

1. Understanding Community Resilience — 1

Part 1

2. The Role Of Social Workers In Building Resilience — 7

Part 2

3. Assessment Tools For Community Needs — 13

Part 3

4. Designing Inclusive Programs — 19

Part 4

5. Empowering Vulnerable Populations — 27

Part 5

6. Youth Engagement And Leadership — 35

Part 6

7. Crisis Response And Management — 41

Part 7

8. Mental Health Support Systems — 47

Part 8

9. Economic Development And Sustainability — 53

Part 9

10. Building Social Capital — 61

Part 10

11. Environmental Challenges And Community Resilience — 67

Part 11

12. Education For Resilience — 73

Contents

Part 12

13. Community-Led Initiatives   81

Part 13

14. Collaborations And Partnerships   87

Part 14

15. Technology And Innovation   95

Part 15

16. Legal And Policy Frameworks For Resilience   101

Part 16

17. Cultural Competence In Social Work   107

Part 17

18. Monitoring And Evaluation Of Resilience   113

Part 18

19. Challenges And Barriers To Building Resilience   119

Part 19

20. Future Directions In Community Resilience   125

Part 20

21. SUMMARY   131

Citation and Reference   135

Other Books of the Author   137

Contact   139

PRAYER

"Om Bhadram Karnebhih Shrinuyama Devah
Bhadram Pashyemakshabhiryajatrah
Sthirairangais Tushtuvamsastanubhih
Vyashema Devahitam Yadayuh
Svasti Na Indro Vriddhashravah
Svasti Nah Pusha Vishwavedah
Svasti Nastarkshyo Arishtanemih
Svasti No Brihaspatir Dadhatu
Om Shantih Shantih Shantih"

This mantra is a prayer for universal well-being, invoking the blessings of various deities for protection, health, and happiness. It emphasizes the importance of experiencing the auspicious through all senses and living a life aligned with divine purpose. The repetition of "Shantih" at the end signifies a deep desire for peace in the individual, the environment, and the universe at large. This mantra is often recited as a prayer for peace, prosperity, and the physical and spiritual well-being of all beings.

About the Author

Dr. Minakshi Bansal, born in the bustling metropolis of Delhi, India, has led a life steeped in artistry, scholarly pursuit, and an unwavering commitment to societal betterment. Following her marriage, she relocated to Ahmedabad, Gujarat, where she has since blossomed into a multifaceted beacon of inspiration for many. Dr. Minakshi is not only recognized as a gifted artist in the realm of Fine Arts but also as an esteemed author, a devoted social worker and a dedicated research scholar in Psychology. Her journey, marked by a profound dedication to elevating those around her, especially the downtrodden and underprivileged children of society, is a testament to her deep-seated belief in the transformative power of engagement and empathy.

From her earliest days, Minakshi was distinguished by an insatiable appetite for reading. Her literary universe was inhabited by characters and narratives that spanned ethical tales, motivational and inspirational stories, and the mythic parables imbued with life lessons. This voracious reading habit was not merely for personal edification but was driven by a desire to distill and disseminate the essence of these narratives to foster the development of students and peers alike. She was particularly captivated by the lives and teachings of historical figures and spiritual leaders such as Adi Shankaracharya, Swami Vivekananda, Dr. APJ Abdul Kalam, Mahamana Pandit Madan Mohan Malviya, Mahatma Gandhi, Sardar Vallabhai Patel, and Vinoba Bhave, among others. Their philosophies and life stories fueled her ambition to embody their ideals of resilience, selflessness, and relentless pursuit of knowledge.

Dr. Minakshi's academic and practical engagement with psychology has been equally noteworthy. As a research scholar, her focus has been on exploring the intricate tapestry of the human psyche, aiming to unlock the potential for psychological well-being and societal harmony. Her scholarly work is complemented by her active involvement in social work, where she employs her academic insights to make tangible differences in the lives of the underprivileged. Her endeavours in social work are characterized by an innovative approach that combines traditional wisdom with contemporary psychological practices to address the multifaceted challenges faced by these communities.

Her artistic talents, another facet of her diverse capabilities, are not merely a personal passion but also serve as a medium through which she communicates and connects with others. Her art, rich in symbolism and emotional depth, reflects her philosophical inquiries and social concerns, offering viewers a glimpse into the breadth of her intellect and the depth of her compassion.

In addition to her contributions to the arts and social sciences, Dr. Minakshi has embraced the healing arts of Pranic Healing, mastering the techniques developed by Master Choa Kok Sui. This practice, which focuses on the manipulation of Prana or life energy to heal the body and aura, has been both a personal journey of discovery and a means through which she extends her healing touch to others. Her proficiency in Pranic Healing is complemented by her advocacy and teaching of various forms of meditation aimed at rejuvenation, personal betterment, and the cultivation of harmony within individuals and communities alike.

Dr. Minakshi's life is a narrative of relentless pursuit, not just of personal achievement but of the upliftment and empowerment of society at large. Her diverse interests and talents—spanning the arts, literature, psychology, and the healing practices—converge on a singular path of service. She embodies the spirit of the luminaries who inspired her, channelling their legacy through her actions and teachings. Through her books, art, and social initiatives, she continues to inspire a new generation to embark on their own journeys of self-discovery, resilience, and altruism.

Her commitment to social betterment, particularly her focus on uplifting underprivileged children, reflects a deep understanding of the transformative potential of education and personal development. By integrating her knowledge of psychology, her artistic sensibilities, and her healing practices, Dr. Bansal has developed a holistic approach to social work that addresses both the immediate needs and the long-term well-being of the communities she serves.

As an author, Dr. Minakshi's writings offer a blend of inspirational insights, practical wisdom, and reflective contemplations drawn from her extensive reading and life experiences. Her books serve as a guide for those seeking to navigate the complexities of life with grace, resilience, and purpose. Through her narratives, she extends an invitation to her readers to explore the depths of their own potential and to contribute meaningfully to the collective well-being of society.

In Dr. Minakshi Bansal, we find a remarkable synthesis of the artist, the scholar, the healer, and the social activist. Her life's work stands as a beacon of hope and a source of inspiration for individuals seeking to make a difference in the world. Her story is a compelling reminder of the power of individual action, rooted in compassion and driven by a profound commitment to the betterment of humanity. Dr. Minakshi's legacy is not just in the tangible outcomes of her efforts but in the enduring spirit of inquiry, empathy, and service that she embodies.

Preface

In the rapidly changing landscapes of our communities, resilience has become a buzzword not just for its relevance but for its necessity. The world we live in today presents a tapestry of challenges—environmental, social, economic, and beyond—that require not only immediate responses but also forward-thinking strategies to secure a sustainable future. This preface serves as an entryway into an exploration of what it means to build and nurture resilient communities that can withstand, adapt to, and recover from the adversities they face.

The journey toward understanding and cultivating resilience is multidimensional. It requires a comprehensive approach that blends theory with practice, knowledge with action, and individual effort with collective power. The essence of resilience lies not merely in surviving but thriving—transforming challenges into opportunities and adversities into catalysts for growth and innovation.

In the realm of social work and community planning, resilience takes on a particularly poignant role. Social workers stand on the front lines, grappling with the immediate human realities and consequences of crises. Their work, however, extends far beyond crisis response; it is about embedding strength and sustainability into the fabric of communities. Through their eyes, we see not just the vulnerabilities but also the immense capacities of communities to rise above their challenges.

Resilience is deeply personal yet overwhelmingly communal. It is about the individual who recovers from a setback with renewed strength and the neighborhood that bands together to create a robust support system. It is about cities that rebuild smarter and stronger infrastructure after a disaster and about global communities that share knowledge and resources to tackle universal challenges like climate change.

This exploration is grounded in the belief that every community, regardless of its size or location, holds the seeds of its own resilience. It is through nurturing these seeds—by applying the right knowledge, tools, and resources—that communities can flourish. This belief is supported by a myriad of stories from around the world, where innovative approaches and tireless community efforts have painted vivid pictures of resilience.

However, building resilience is not without its challenges. Resources can be scarce, policies may be restrictive, and inherent social and economic inequalities often complicate efforts. Moreover, the unpredictable nature of many modern challenges, such as the increasing frequency and severity of natural disasters and pandemics, adds layers of complexity to resilience-building initiatives.

Against this backdrop, the role of social workers and community leaders becomes even more critical. They are not only providers of aid or services but also advocates, educators, and catalysts for change. Their work in understanding community dynamics, advocating for equitable policies, and implementing innovative solutions is vital for fostering environments where resilience can thrive.

The narratives shared in this context are both a reflection of past endeavors and a map for future efforts. They highlight the importance of adaptability, the power of community involvement, and the impact of technology and innovation in reshaping our approaches to community resilience. Each story, each example, each piece of research discussed serves as a stepping stone toward more robust and resilient communities.

As we move forward, it becomes clear that the task of building resilience is unending and ever-evolving. It demands continuous learning, adaptation, and collective action. It requires us to rethink traditional methods, to challenge existing frameworks, and to be open to new ideas and collaborations. The path to resilience is as much about using proven strategies as it is about pioneering new ones.

In this regard, the insights offered here are intended to spark dialogue, inspire action, and encourage a deeper commitment to cultivating resilience at all levels of society. Whether you are a social worker, a policy maker, a community leader, or a concerned citizen, the discussions contained in these pages aim to equip you with both the vision and the practical tools needed to make a tangible difference in your communities.

Ultimately, the pursuit of resilience is a shared journey—a collective endeavor that transcends geographical, cultural, and social boundaries. It is a commitment to a future where communities not only bounce back but also bounce forward, stronger and more unified than before. Let this be a call to action, an invitation to step forward and contribute to the vital work of building resilient communities.

Dr. Minakshi Bansal
Social Activist
Ahmedabad, Gujarat, Bharat

I
Understanding Community Resilience

Community resilience is a critical concept in understanding how populations adapt to various stressors and disturbances, ranging from economic hardship and social disruptions to natural disasters and environmental changes. The essence of community resilience lies in the ability of communities to rebound from adversity, adapt to new circumstances, and even progress despite challenges. This broad understanding lays the groundwork for more detailed examination and application in social work and community planning.

Defining Community Resilience

At its core, community resilience refers to the sustained ability of a community to utilize available resources to respond to, withstand, and recover from adverse situations. This resilience encompasses a range of elements, from the physical and economic to the social and cultural. It is not merely the capacity to bounce back to a pre-disaster state but also to learn from the experience and integrate those lessons into community practices and policies for better future outcomes.

The concept of resilience can be broken down into several key components, including robustness, which is the ability to maintain core functions without degradation; redundancy, which involves having backup resources to compensate for system failures; resourcefulness, which relates to the capacity to apply material and human resources to meet challenges; and rapidity, which concerns the speed with which a community can recover functionality.

Theoretical Frameworks Underpinning Community Resilience

Several theories contribute to our understanding of community resilience. One of the foundational theories is the ecological resilience theory, which originally comes from the field of ecology but has been applied to social systems. This theory emphasizes adaptability and transformability in systems, suggesting that resilient communities are not only adaptable in the face of short-term disturbances but also capable of transforming their structures and functions in response to long-term changes in their environment.

Another significant theoretical perspective is the psychosocial resilience approach, which focuses on the mental and social aspects of community resilience. This approach considers the attitudes, beliefs, and collective behaviors of community members that contribute to their ability to handle stress and rebuild community life.

Systems theory also plays a crucial role in understanding community resilience by highlighting the interconnectedness of various community functions and the complex interactions between different social, economic, and environmental factors.

According to systems theory, a change in one part of the community can have ripple effects throughout the system, influencing the community's overall resilience.

Applying Resilience Concepts to Community Settings

To effectively apply the concept of community resilience, it is essential for social workers and community planners to engage in comprehensive community assessment processes. These assessments help identify the strengths and vulnerabilities within a community and determine the most effective strategies for enhancing resilience. For instance, a community might have strong social networks that can be leveraged to improve communication and resource distribution during times of crisis, but it might lack economic diversity, which could exacerbate the impact of job losses in a single sector.

Community resilience is also deeply tied to the concept of social capital, which refers to the networks of relationships among people who live and work in a particular society, enabling that society to function effectively. Social capital can be a tremendous asset in enhancing community resilience by fostering trust, mutual assistance, and shared responsibilities, which are crucial in times of crisis.

Challenges in Building Community Resilience

Despite the apparent benefits of fostering community resilience, there are numerous challenges. These include economic constraints, political inertia, social inequalities, and the complexities of coordinating across various sectors and organizations. Additionally, the increasing frequency and intensity of global challenges, such as climate change and pandemics, complicate efforts to build and sustain resilience.

Social workers play a pivotal role in overcoming these challenges by advocating for inclusive and equitable resilience-building practices that address the needs of all community members, particularly the most vulnerable. They also facilitate collaboration among government agencies, non-profits, and community groups to marshal resources and knowledge effectively.

Understanding and enhancing community resilience is a multifaceted endeavor that requires robust theoretical knowledge, practical skills, and a committed approach to social equity and justice. As communities worldwide face an array of challenges, the concept of resilience remains a beacon guiding the efforts of those dedicated to creating sustainable and thriving societies.

"Resilience isn't just about weathering the storm; it's about learning to dance in the rain. Every drop teaches us, every challenge refines us. In the rhythms of adversity, we discover our strength."

ജ

II

The Role of Social Workers in Building Resilience

Social workers play a crucial role in fostering community resilience, serving as the connective tissue that binds together various social services, community resources, and policy initiatives. Their involvement spans from direct intervention and advocacy to the planning and implementation of programs that strengthen the socio-economic fabrics of communities. This broad spectrum of activities highlights the central role that social workers occupy in building resilience at community levels.

Facilitating Community Engagement and Empowerment

One of the primary roles of social workers in building resilience is to facilitate community engagement. They act as catalysts for empowering residents to take an active part in developing solutions to their challenges. By promoting community-based decision-making, social workers help ensure that the interventions are culturally appropriate and tailored to the specific needs and resources of the community. This approach not only improves the effectiveness of the initiatives but also builds a sense of ownership among community members, which is crucial for the sustainability of resilience efforts.

Empowerment through social work involves equipping individuals and groups with the skills and knowledge needed to effect change in their communities. Social workers conduct workshops and training sessions on topics like financial literacy, disaster preparedness, and conflict resolution. These educational efforts enhance the capacity of community members to navigate and manage crises, thereby directly contributing to the resilience of the community.

Advocacy and Policy Influence

Social workers also play an integral role as advocates for vulnerable populations. Their deep understanding of the challenges faced by different community segments enables them to advocate for policies that promote social justice and equity. By lobbying for changes in legislation that address the root causes of vulnerability, such as poverty, discrimination, and lack of access to services, social workers help to create a more resilient social environment.

This advocacy extends to ensuring that community voices are heard in the halls of power, promoting policies that support resilience-building measures such as improved housing, access to quality healthcare, and environmental sustainability. Social workers often collaborate with policymakers to draft and implement these policies, ensuring they are grounded in the real-world needs and experiences of the communities they serve.

Direct Crisis Intervention

In times of crisis, social workers are often on the front lines, providing immediate support and intervention. They assess the needs of individuals and communities, coordinate with emergency services, and facilitate access to disaster relief resources. Following initial crisis response efforts, social workers remain involved in long-term recovery processes, helping individuals and communities rebuild and recover from traumatic events.

Their role in crisis intervention is not only about managing the aftermath but also about preparing communities for future challenges. Social workers implement programs that enhance the community's capacity to respond to and recover from future disasters, thus building a foundation of resilience that sustains over time.

Developing and Leading Resilience Programs

Beyond direct intervention, social workers are instrumental in designing and leading programs that build community resilience. They utilize their expertise in social dynamics and community needs assessment to develop initiatives that address specific vulnerabilities within the community. These programs might focus on enhancing economic stability, improving mental health support, or increasing educational opportunities, depending on the identified needs.

Social workers often oversee the implementation of these programs, managing teams, securing funding, and evaluating the outcomes. This leadership role is vital not only in the execution of resilience-building activities but also in demonstrating the effectiveness and value of such initiatives to stakeholders and funding bodies.

Networking and Collaboration

Another vital aspect of the social worker's role in building resilience is networking and collaboration. No single sector or professional group can build community resilience alone; it requires a concerted effort across various sectors. Social workers facilitate this collaboration, bringing together government agencies, non-profit organizations, community leaders, and residents to forge effective partnerships.

These collaborations are crucial for sharing resources, information, and best practices. They also allow for the pooling of resources to address significant challenges more effectively and ensure that efforts are not duplicated but rather strategically aligned to maximize impact.

In essence, social workers are central to the development and maintenance of community resilience. Through their varied roles—facilitating community engagement, advocating for policy change, providing crisis intervention, leading resilience programs, and fostering collaboration—they help to weave the fabric of resilient communities. Their work ensures that communities are not only prepared to face current and future challenges but are also equipped to thrive in the face of adversity.

"Community resilience is a tapestry woven from the threads of shared struggles and collective strength. Each thread strengthens the fabric, each story enriches the narrative. Together, we build a quilt that shelters all from the storms."

⚮

III

Assessment Tools for Community Needs

Assessing the needs of a community is an essential step in developing strategies that enhance resilience. Social workers, community planners, and local leaders use a variety of assessment tools to understand the specific challenges and resources available within a community. These tools provide critical data that inform the design of interventions aimed at improving community well-being and resilience. This understanding helps to tailor responses to the unique contexts of different communities, ensuring that resilience-building efforts are effective and sustainable.

Survey Instruments

One of the primary tools used in community needs assessments are surveys. Surveys can be designed to gather quantitative data on a wide range of topics, including health, employment, education, housing, and access to services. They provide valuable insights into the demographic characteristics of a community, the needs of its members, and the gaps in services that might exist. By carefully crafting questions that explore different aspects of community life, social workers can gather comprehensive data that informs all stages of program development and implementation.

Surveys are often administered through household visits, community meetings, or online platforms, depending on the community's access to technology and the resources available for the assessment process. The design of the survey must consider cultural sensitivities and linguistic diversity to ensure that the data collected is representative of the entire community.

Focus Groups

Focus groups are another essential tool in the community assessment toolkit. They involve gathering small groups of community members to discuss specific issues or areas of concern. These discussions are facilitated by social workers or researchers who guide the conversation through a series of open-ended questions. This qualitative method allows for a deeper understanding of the issues that surveys might identify only superficially.

The value of focus groups lies in their ability to uncover detailed insights about the community's perceptions, experiences, and ideas for potential solutions. They are particularly useful for exploring sensitive issues that may not be fully captured through surveys, such as community dynamics, experiences with discrimination, or personal stories of resilience.

Asset Mapping

Asset mapping is a tool that identifies the strengths and resources of a community. Unlike methods that focus primarily on needs and deficits, asset mapping looks at what is working well in a community and what resources are available that can be leveraged to address challenges. This approach not only highlights existing assets such as schools, hospitals, community centers, and local businesses but also identifies the skills, knowledge, and abilities of community members.

Asset mapping involves various stakeholders in the community, including local businesses, service providers, residents, and government agencies. The process fosters a sense of community pride and ownership over the development process, as it empowers community members by focusing on their strengths rather than just their needs.

Geographic Information Systems (GIS)

Geographic Information Systems (GIS) are increasingly used in community needs assessments to provide a spatial analysis of community data. GIS can map out demographic information, economic data, environmental conditions, and access to services, overlaying this information to identify patterns and trends that might not be evident from non-spatial data.

For example, GIS can help identify areas within a community that lack access to public transportation or are far from healthcare facilities. This tool is invaluable in planning for resilient infrastructure and services, as it allows for precise targeting of interventions and can significantly enhance the efficiency and effectiveness of resource allocation.

Community Forums

Community forums are public meetings where residents and stakeholders come together to discuss community issues, needs, and opportunities. These forums provide a platform for open communication between community members and those in positions of authority, such as local government officials, social workers, and service providers. They are an excellent tool for building consensus and for encouraging community involvement in decision-making processes.

During these forums, participants can voice their concerns, ask questions, and provide feedback on proposed plans and programs. This direct engagement helps ensure that community needs assessments are not only inclusive but also accurately reflect the priorities and desires of the community.

In summary, a comprehensive community needs assessment relies on a combination of tools and methods to gather a wide range of data. Surveys, focus groups, asset mapping, GIS, and community forums each play a role in painting a detailed picture of community needs and resources. By effectively using these tools, social workers and community leaders can develop tailored, sustainable, and effective resilience-building strategies that truly meet the needs of the communities they serve.

"In the garden of community, every hand that plants a seed strengthens a bond. Each plant that grows is a testament to what can be achieved together. This is how resilience is cultivated—from the ground up, with patience and persistence."

IV
Designing Inclusive Programs

Designing inclusive programs is a fundamental aspect of community development and resilience building. Inclusive programs ensure that all community members, regardless of their socio-economic status, ethnicity, age, gender, or abilities, have access to the resources and opportunities necessary to thrive. The process of creating such programs requires a deliberate focus on equity, participation, and the specific needs of diverse groups within the community.

Understanding Community Diversity

Before designing any program, it is crucial to understand the diversity within the community. This involves recognizing and mapping the varied needs, barriers, and resources that different groups face. Diversity in communities encompasses a wide range of factors, including but not limited to race, ethnicity, gender identity, age, economic status, disabilities, and cultural backgrounds. Each group may have unique challenges and strengths that must be considered in program design to avoid one-size-fits-all solutions that do not adequately address or could inadvertently marginalize some community members.

Social workers and program designers use tools like demographic analysis, needs assessments, and community consultations to gather detailed information about the composition and needs of the community. This data serves as the foundation for developing programs that are genuinely inclusive and equitable.

Engaging Stakeholders and Community Participation

Stakeholder engagement is key to designing inclusive programs. This involves including representatives from all community segments, especially those who are often underrepresented, in the planning and decision-making processes. Engaging stakeholders not only helps in gathering diverse perspectives but also builds a sense of ownership among community members, enhancing the sustainability of the programs.

Community participation can take many forms, such as public forums, focus groups, advisory committees, and participatory action research. Each of these methods provides opportunities for community members to voice their opinions, suggest solutions, and influence program design directly. This participatory approach ensures that the programs are not only inclusive but also aligned with the community's values and needs.

Addressing Systemic Barriers

Inclusive programming must also focus on identifying and addressing systemic barriers that prevent equal participation and access to resources. These barriers can be legal, cultural, economic, or political and often disproportionately affect certain groups. For instance, language barriers, lack of physical accessibility, and cultural insensitivity can exclude non-native speakers, people with disabilities, and ethnic minorities from fully participating in social programs.

To overcome these barriers, programs must include specific measures such as offering materials in multiple languages, ensuring physical accessibility, and providing cultural competency training for staff and volunteers. Moreover, policies and practices should be scrutinized and revised to eliminate biases and systemic obstacles that hinder inclusion.

Flexible and Adaptive Program Design

Inclusive programs are flexible and capable of adapting to changing community needs and circumstances. This adaptability is crucial in maintaining relevance and effectiveness, particularly in diverse communities where needs can vary widely and change over time. Program designers should build in regular review cycles and feedback mechanisms to assess the impact of the programs and make necessary adjustments.

Adaptive program design also means that the programs can respond to unforeseen challenges or opportunities. For example, during a crisis like a pandemic, programs might need to shift from in-person to virtual formats. Programs that are designed with flexibility in mind can quickly adapt to such changes without significantly disrupting service delivery.

Training and Capacity Building

To effectively implement inclusive programs, there is a need for ongoing training and capacity building for those involved in program delivery. This includes training in cultural competency, anti-discrimination practices, and specific skills related to accessibility and inclusivity. Equipping staff, volunteers, and community leaders with the knowledge and skills to manage diverse groups ensures that the programs are delivered effectively and respectfully.

Training should also extend to community members, particularly those from marginalized groups, to strengthen their capacity to engage with and benefit from the programs. This might include leadership training, educational workshops, and other capacity-building initiatives that empower community members to take active roles in their community's development.

Monitoring and Evaluation

Finally, robust monitoring and evaluation mechanisms are essential to ensuring the inclusiveness and effectiveness of social programs. These mechanisms should specifically measure how well the programs meet the needs of diverse community groups and identify areas where improvements are needed. Feedback from community members, particularly those who are direct beneficiaries of the programs, should be a central component of the evaluation process.

Inclusive programs are not static; they evolve based on continuous learning and feedback. By systematically collecting and analyzing data on program outcomes and community satisfaction, program designers can ensure that the programs remain responsive and effective at promoting inclusion and equity within the community.

Designing inclusive programs requires a comprehensive approach that considers the complexities and diversities of community populations. By focusing on equitable participation, addressing systemic barriers, ensuring flexibility, providing appropriate training, and implementing effective monitoring, social workers and community developers can create programs that genuinely cater to all community members, thereby fostering a more resilient and inclusive community.

&

• 23 •

"Every crisis faced together is a lesson in the power of unity. Every challenge overcome is a victory not just for one, but for all. For in unity, there is strength that can conquer even the mightiest of adversities."

෴

V
Empowering Vulnerable Populations

Empowering vulnerable populations is essential for building community resilience. Vulnerable groups, including the elderly, disabled, and economically disadvantaged, often face systemic barriers that limit their access to resources and opportunities, exacerbating their vulnerability in times of crisis.

Effective empowerment strategies can help these groups strengthen their capacities, enhance their independence, and improve their overall well-being. The goal is to ensure that resilience-building efforts are inclusive, addressing the needs and potentials of all community members.

Identifying Vulnerable Groups and Understanding Their Needs

The first step in empowering vulnerable populations is to accurately identify who these groups are within the community and understand their specific needs and challenges. This involves more than just recognizing obvious vulnerabilities; it requires a deep dive into the lived experiences of these individuals. Social workers and community leaders must engage directly with these populations through interviews, surveys, and focus groups to gather detailed insights.

This direct engagement is crucial for tailoring empowerment strategies that are genuinely effective and responsive to the needs of the individuals.

For the elderly, issues might include physical mobility, healthcare access, and social isolation. For the disabled, barriers could be related to physical accessibility, employment, and discriminatory attitudes. Economically disadvantaged groups might struggle with housing security, access to quality education, and employment opportunities.

Understanding these nuances allows for the design of targeted interventions that address specific vulnerabilities.

Enhancing Social and Economic Inclusion

Empowerment often starts with improving social and economic inclusion. This can be achieved through programs designed to integrate vulnerable populations into the broader community and economy. For instance, job training programs can be tailored to the skills and capabilities of disabled individuals, or flexible work arrangements can be promoted to accommodate the unique needs of the elderly. Similarly, initiatives that support entrepreneurship can be directed towards economically disadvantaged groups, providing them with the tools and capital necessary to start their own businesses.

Social inclusion is equally important. Community centers, recreational programs, and social events should be accessible to all, including appropriate accommodations for the elderly and disabled. Creating opportunities for social interaction helps mitigate the risks of isolation and depression, particularly for older adults.

Access to Healthcare and Support Services

Access to healthcare is a critical aspect of empowerment. Vulnerable populations often have specific health needs that require regular attention and care. Establishing community healthcare services that are accessible and affordable for all community members is vital. This might involve mobile health clinics, subsidized healthcare programs, or partnerships with local hospitals and health professionals to provide targeted health services at reduced costs.

Support services such as counseling, legal aid, and financial advice should also be made readily available to vulnerable groups. These services play a crucial role in empowering individuals by providing them with the knowledge and support needed to navigate their challenges effectively.

For instance, legal aid can help economically disadvantaged individuals understand and assert their rights, while financial counseling can assist them in managing their finances more effectively, thus reducing economic vulnerability.

Building Capacities and Self-Reliance

Empowerment strategies must also focus on building the capacities and self-reliance of vulnerable populations. This includes education and training programs that are tailored to the needs and abilities of these groups. For example, digital literacy training can be crucial for the elderly, helping them access online services and stay connected with their communities. Similarly, life skills training for disabled individuals can enhance their ability to live independently.

Mentorship programs can also play a significant role in capacity building. By pairing individuals from vulnerable groups with mentors who can provide guidance, support, and encouragement, these programs help individuals build confidence and develop necessary skills for personal and professional growth.

Community Advocacy and Legal Protection

Advocacy is another powerful tool for empowering vulnerable populations. Social workers and community advocates can help raise awareness about the challenges faced by these groups and lobby for policy changes that address their needs. This includes advocating for better housing conditions, anti-discrimination laws, and enhanced social services.

Legal protection is also crucial, as it ensures that vulnerable populations have the same rights as other community members. Strengthening legal frameworks to protect these rights and ensuring that these laws are enforced can significantly empower these individuals by providing them with a secure environment in which to thrive.

Continuous Engagement and Feedback

Lastly, continuous engagement with vulnerable populations is essential to ensure that empowerment strategies remain effective and relevant. This means regularly soliciting feedback from these groups about the programs and services they receive and making adjustments based on their input. Such ongoing engagement not only helps in fine-tuning the initiatives but also reinforces the sense of agency among these populations.

Empowering vulnerable populations requires a multi-faceted

approach that addresses both immediate needs and long-term resilience. By focusing on social and economic inclusion, healthcare access, capacity building, advocacy, and continuous engagement, communities can enhance the resilience and well-being of their most vulnerable members.

This not only benefits these individuals directly but also strengthens the entire community, creating a more inclusive, supportive, and resilient environment for all.

"Social workers are the architects of hope, building bridges over the floods of despair. Their tools are compassion and understanding, their blueprints are resilience and care. In every heart they touch, a foundation of strength is laid."

৪৩

VI
Youth Engagement and Leadership

Engaging youth in resilience-building efforts is essential for fostering a sustainable future and developing the next generation of leaders. Young people bring unique perspectives, innovation, and energy to the challenges their communities face. By actively involving them in planning and decision-making processes, communities can harness these qualities effectively. Furthermore, cultivating leadership skills among young individuals prepares them to handle future challenges adeptly, ensuring that the community's resilience strengthens over time.

The Value of Youth Engagement

Youth engagement in community resilience involves more than just inviting young people to participate; it requires integrating their ideas and perspectives into the very fabric of community planning and problem-solving. Young people are often more aware of, and sensitive to, new and emerging trends, especially in technology and culture, which can be pivotal in addressing modern challenges. By engaging youth, communities can tap into contemporary approaches and innovative solutions that older generations might overlook.

Moreover, young people are likely to experience the long-term consequences of current policies and community decisions more acutely than their older counterparts. Therefore, their involvement ensures that these decisions are forward-looking and sustainable. Engaging youth also helps instill a sense of responsibility and belonging, which is crucial for nurturing future community leaders.

Fostering Youth Leadership

Developing leadership skills among young people is crucial for community resilience. Leadership development involves teaching skills such as critical thinking, problem-solving, effective communication, and collaborative teamwork. These skills are essential for young leaders to influence their peers and drive community projects.

Programs designed to foster youth leadership often include mentorship components, where experienced leaders guide young individuals through the complexities of managing projects and navigating community dynamics. These programs might also offer leadership roles within smaller projects as stepping stones, giving young people a taste of responsibility under supervision before they undertake larger initiatives.

Creating Opportunities for Participation

For youth engagement to be effective, there must be ample and varied opportunities for participation. This could mean involving youth in community planning meetings, having them lead specific projects, or including them in decision-making councils or boards. Schools, local youth organizations, and community centers can serve as hubs for these activities, providing a platform for young people to voice their opinions and learn about civic responsibility.

Opportunities for involvement should also be diverse to cater to different interests and talents. For example, while some youth might be interested in direct political engagement, others might prefer to contribute through art, technology, or environmental conservation efforts. By providing a broad range of engagement pathways, communities can ensure that all young people have the chance to contribute in ways that resonate with their personal passions and skills.

Integrating Technology and Innovation

Leveraging technology is another critical aspect of involving youth in resilience-building. Young people are often adept at using new technologies and are likely to be early adopters of innovative tools and platforms. Communities can utilize this aptitude by encouraging youth to develop or lead projects that employ technology to solve local issues. For instance, initiatives like developing community apps that report local issues, creating digital platforms for community engagement, or using social media to increase awareness and drive community initiatives.

These tech-focused projects not only solve real problems but also provide young people with practical experience in managing technology-driven projects, thus preparing them for leadership roles in an increasingly digital world.

Challenges to Youth Engagement

Despite the benefits, there are challenges to effectively engaging youth in community resilience efforts. These include a lack of resources, limited access to decision-making platforms, and the potential for generational gaps in communication. To overcome these challenges, community leaders and policymakers must be committed to creating structures and processes that facilitate meaningful youth involvement.

This commitment might involve providing funding for youth-led projects, training educators and community leaders on how to work effectively with young people, and establishing clear pathways for youth to express their views and have them taken seriously at the decision-making level.

Evaluating and Adapting Youth Engagement Strategies

To ensure that youth engagement strategies remain effective and relevant, continuous evaluation and adaptation are necessary. Feedback mechanisms should be put in place to gather young people's insights about the engagement processes and the challenges they face. This feedback can then be used to refine and improve the strategies, ensuring that they meet the evolving needs of young people and the broader community.

By involving young people in resilience-building efforts and fostering their leadership skills, communities not only empower the next generation but also enhance their capacity to face future challenges. This dual focus on engagement and skill development ensures that young people are not only prepared to lead in the future but are also capable of contributing effectively in the present, driving community initiatives that are innovative, inclusive, and forward-thinking.

"True resilience emanates from a community that values every voice. It thrives where diversity is celebrated and differences are bridges, not barriers. Here, every individual is a vital thread in the fabric of society."

଼ଅ

VII

Crisis Response and Management

Crisis response and management are critical components of social work, requiring swift and effective action to mitigate the impacts of emergencies on vulnerable populations. Social workers play a pivotal role in these situations, providing support, resources, and guidance to individuals and communities affected by crises. Their involvement is essential for managing the immediate aftermath of an emergency as well as for the long-term recovery and resilience-building that follows.

Preparedness and Early Intervention

Effective crisis management begins with preparedness. Social workers, in collaboration with emergency services and community organizations, develop and implement crisis response plans that outline specific roles and responsibilities before a crisis occurs. This proactive approach includes training programs for social workers and community leaders, development of communication strategies to alert and inform the public, and establishment of resource centers that can quickly provide necessary supplies and services during a crisis.

Early intervention is another key component of effective crisis response. Social workers strive to identify and mitigate risks by providing support services before situations escalate into full-blown crises. For instance, in communities prone to natural disasters, social workers can facilitate educational programs on disaster preparedness, ensuring that residents know how to respond in the event of an emergency. This preparation helps minimize panic and confusion, enabling a more organized and effective response when a crisis does occur.

Rapid Response Teams

When a crisis strikes, rapid response teams comprising social workers and other emergency personnel are often among the first to react. These teams are trained to assess the situation quickly, provide immediate assistance, and coordinate with other services to ensure a comprehensive response. The presence of social workers in these teams is crucial, as they bring a unique understanding of the psychosocial dynamics that play a significant role in how individuals and communities react to and recover from traumatic events.

Social workers on rapid response teams focus on critical needs such as ensuring safety, providing psychological first aid, and securing basic necessities like food, water, and shelter. They also play an important role in identifying individuals who are particularly vulnerable, such as the elderly, disabled, and children, and ensuring that these groups receive the targeted support they need.

Resource Distribution and Management

Managing the distribution of resources during a crisis is a complex challenge that requires organized and equitable approaches to ensure that help reaches those most in need. Social workers collaborate with local authorities and organizations to oversee the allocation of resources. They help establish priorities based on immediate needs and vulnerability assessments, ensuring that resources are used effectively to support recovery efforts.

Social workers also monitor and evaluate the impact of resource distribution, adjusting strategies as needed to address gaps in service delivery. This continuous assessment helps to maintain fairness in resource allocation and prevents the exacerbation of existing inequalities during the recovery process.

Communication and Information Dissemination

Effective communication is essential during a crisis. Social workers ensure that accurate and timely information reaches all segments of the community, including non-English speakers and people with disabilities. This involves not only disseminating information through various channels such as social media, local radio, and community bulletins but also organizing community meetings to address concerns and provide updates.

Social workers also serve as a bridge between the community and authorities, conveying community needs and feedback to decision-makers and bringing information back to the public. This two-way communication helps maintain transparency and trust between the community and those managing the crisis.

Psychosocial Support

Beyond physical needs, social workers provide crucial psychosocial support to individuals and communities affected by crises. They offer counseling services, support groups, and other therapeutic activities to help people cope with the trauma and stress of emergency situations. This support is vital for long-term recovery, as unresolved emotional and psychological issues can impede individuals' ability to rebuild their lives and can affect community resilience.

Recovery and Resilience Building

After the immediate crisis has passed, social workers play a key role in the recovery and resilience-building phase. They work with individuals and communities to restore services and infrastructure, support economic recovery, and promote social cohesion. Social workers also advocate for improvements in policies and practices based on lessons learned during the crisis, aiming to strengthen community resilience against future emergencies.

This comprehensive approach ensures that the response to crises is not only about managing the emergency itself but also about laying the groundwork for sustainable recovery and resilience. By focusing on preparedness, rapid response, resource management, effective communication, psychosocial support, and recovery planning, social workers provide essential services that safeguard and enhance the well-being of communities in the face of crises.

"Resilience is more than surviving; it's thriving with passion and purpose. It's not just about bouncing back but also stepping forward into new possibilities. It is a journey of continuous transformation and relentless pursuit of progress."

‽

VIII

Mental Health Support Systems

Establishing robust mental health support systems within communities is essential for helping individuals withstand and recover from adversities. Mental health challenges can significantly impair individual well-being and community cohesion, making the development of effective support systems a critical component of community resilience. These systems are designed to provide preventive care, immediate intervention, and long-term recovery services, ensuring that mental health care is accessible and effective for all community members.

Understanding the Need for Mental Health Support

The first step in establishing mental health support systems is recognizing the widespread impact that mental health issues can have on individuals and communities. Mental health problems do not discriminate; they can affect anyone regardless of age, gender, economic status, or background. However, the risk of developing mental health issues can increase significantly due to various stressors, including economic hardships, social isolation, and after experiencing traumatic events such as natural disasters or community violence.

Effective mental health systems therefore begin with comprehensive community assessments to identify mental health needs and resources. These assessments help pinpoint gaps in services, areas with high incidences of mental health issues, and segments of the population that might be underserved. With this information, planners can design interventions that are specifically tailored to meet the community's unique challenges and leverage its strengths.

Preventive Care and Awareness

Preventive care is a cornerstone of effective mental health support systems. This involves promoting mental health awareness through education and outreach programs that help destigmatize mental illness and encourage individuals to seek help early when they experience mental health issues. Schools, workplaces, and community centers can serve as vital platforms for these educational initiatives.

Programs may include workshops on stress management, the importance of mental health, and the signs of mental health deterioration. Training community leaders and educators to recognize these signs can lead to earlier intervention and support, preventing more severe mental health crises. Additionally, integrating mental health education into school curricula can equip young people with coping mechanisms that will serve them throughout their lives.

Accessible and Responsive Services

Accessibility to mental health services is critical. This means services need to be affordable, timely, and culturally appropriate.

Community-based mental health services, such as counseling centers, hotlines, and mobile health teams, can provide essential support close to where people live. These services should be staffed by professionals trained to handle a variety of mental health issues and should be capable of responding to both individual and collective needs following a crisis.

Telemedicine and online counseling have become increasingly important, especially in underserved or remote areas. These technologies can bridge the gap between mental health professionals and community members, offering real-time support and intervention without the need for travel, which can be a significant barrier to accessing care.

Integration with Other Community Services

For mental health support systems to be effective, they must be integrated with other community services. Collaboration with healthcare providers, social services, educational institutions, and law enforcement ensures that individuals receive comprehensive support that addresses all aspects of their well-being.

For example, integrating mental health services with primary healthcare allows for the early detection and treatment of mental health issues during routine health examinations. Similarly, schools can implement programs that support the emotional and psychological well-being of students, which are critical for educational success.

Support for Caregivers and Families

Caregivers and families play a crucial role in supporting individuals with mental health issues, yet they also need support themselves. Establishing support networks for caregivers—through counseling, respite care, and educational resources—can prevent caregiver burnout and enhance the quality of care they provide. Family education programs can teach coping strategies and ways to effectively support a family member dealing with mental health challenges, fostering a supportive home environment that can accelerate recovery.

Community-Based Recovery Programs

Long-term recovery from mental health issues often requires ongoing support and rehabilitation. Community-based recovery programs that focus on social reintegration and skill development can be particularly effective. These programs might include therapeutic group activities, employment support services, and peer-led support groups, all of which help individuals regain confidence and rebuild their lives after significant mental health challenges.

By fostering a supportive environment through these comprehensive strategies, communities can enhance their resilience and capacity to handle adversities. The establishment of strong mental health support systems not only aids in recovery but also strengthens the community's overall health and cohesion, making it better equipped to face future challenges.

"In the face of adversity, resilience is a symphony played by a community in harmony. Each note resonates with the power of collaboration, each melody sings of shared resilience. Together, they compose a song of enduring strength."

೫

IX

Economic Development and Sustainability

Economic development and sustainability are crucial elements in strengthening community resilience. When communities foster economic systems that prioritize sustainability and resilience, they are better prepared to face and recover from adversities, whether economic downturns, environmental disasters, or social disruptions. Sustainable economic development involves strategies that not only generate economic growth but also ensure that such growth is equitable and environmentally friendly. This comprehensive approach helps create resilient communities that can thrive in the face of various challenges.

Understanding Sustainable Economic Development

Sustainable economic development seeks to balance economic growth with the need to protect the environment and ensure social equity. It involves initiatives that do not deplete resources but rather use them in a way that maintains their availability for future generations. This approach also includes efforts to reduce inequalities, ensuring that the benefits of economic growth are widely shared across all segments of the community.

Key to understanding sustainable economic development is recognizing that long-term prosperity depends on a healthy environment and a stable, inclusive society. This perspective shifts the focus from short-term gains to long-term goals that benefit the entire community, fostering resilience through economic practices that are robust, inclusive, and environmentally sustainable.

Diversifying the Local Economy

Economic diversification is a vital strategy in building resilience. Communities that rely on a single industry or sector are more vulnerable to economic shocks. Diversifying the local economy can involve developing new industries, supporting small and medium enterprises (SMEs), and promoting entrepreneurship in various sectors, including technology, services, and green industries.

Investments in education and training programs are crucial to diversifying the economy. These programs can equip the local workforce with the skills needed in emerging sectors, such as renewable energy, digital technology, and sustainable agriculture. By fostering a skilled workforce, communities can attract a broader range of business investments and reduce their vulnerability to economic downturns in any single sector.

Supporting Small and Medium Enterprises (SMEs)

SMEs are often described as the backbone of resilient economies because they are major employers and can be highly adaptive to changing market conditions. Supporting these enterprises through access to finance, business mentorship programs, and subsidies for adopting sustainable practices can stimulate local economic growth while enhancing resilience.

Initiatives such as microfinance, credit guarantees, and business incubators can provide SMEs with the resources they need to start and grow. These supports are particularly important in communities where large-scale industrial investments are scarce or where such investments would not align with the community's sustainable development goals.

Promoting Sustainable Agricultural Practices

Agriculture not only provides food and employment in many communities but also plays a crucial role in the sustainability of local and global ecosystems. Promoting sustainable agricultural practices helps ensure food security, supports rural economies, and reduces environmental impact. Practices such as permaculture, organic farming, and agroforestry are examples of how agriculture can contribute to sustainable economic development.

Governments and community organizations can support sustainable agriculture through policies that encourage organic farming, protect critical habitats, and provide farmers with access to markets for their sustainable products. Education and training programs can also help farmers adopt practices that are both environmentally friendly and economically viable.

Investing in Renewable Energy

Transitioning to renewable energy sources like solar, wind, and hydroelectric power is another key component of sustainable economic development. This transition not only reduces dependency on fossil fuels but also creates job opportunities in new and expanding sectors. Investing in renewable energy infrastructure can stimulate local economies, reduce energy costs, and decrease environmental pollutants.

Community-based renewable energy projects can empower local residents, providing them with direct benefits from energy production and consumption. These projects can also serve as educational and demonstrational hubs for sustainable practices, spreading the benefits of renewable energy throughout the community.

Developing Green Infrastructure

Green infrastructure, such as parks, green roofs, and urban forests, provides multiple economic and environmental benefits. These include reducing urban heat, managing stormwater, improving air quality, and providing recreational spaces for residents. Investing in green infrastructure is an investment in the community's health, well-being, and economic resilience.

Policies that promote green infrastructure development can also stimulate local economies through job creation in construction, maintenance, and environmental management. These jobs often require new skills and training, providing further opportunities for economic development within the community.

Fostering Economic Resilience Through Community Involvement

Finally, sustainable economic development relies on the active involvement of the community. This means engaging local stakeholders in planning and decision-making processes to ensure that economic development initiatives align with the community's needs and values. Community involvement helps build a sense of ownership and commitment to sustainable practices, which is essential for long-term resilience.

By focusing on strategies that promote economic diversification, support SMEs, encourage sustainable agricultural and energy practices, invest in green infrastructure, and engage community members, communities can build economic systems that are not only productive but also resilient and sustainable. These efforts ensure that economic development contributes to a stable and healthy environment, equitable opportunities for all, and the overall resilience of the community.

"The roots of community resilience lie deep in the soil of understanding and empathy. When nurtured by social workers and community leaders, these roots grow into a tree that stands firm, no matter how fierce the storms may be."

೮೦

X
Building Social Capital

Social capital plays a critical role in enhancing the resilience of communities. It refers to the networks of relationships among people who live and work in a particular society, enabling that society to function effectively. Social capital is built on the foundations of trust, reciprocity, and mutual aid, and it significantly influences how communities respond to and recover from adversities. By fostering strong, cooperative relationships among residents, communities can enhance their capacity to manage crises, support vulnerable populations, and implement effective recovery strategies.

Understanding Social Capital

Social capital is composed of three main components: bonding, bridging, and linking social capital. Bonding social capital refers to the ties between family members and close friends who provide emotional support and assistance in times of need. Bridging social capital encompasses more distant relationships, such as those between acquaintances and colleagues, which can offer new information and broader perspectives. Linking social capital involves connections between individuals and people in positions of power, such as government officials or business leaders, facilitating access to external resources and support.

Each type of social capital plays a unique role in resilience-building. Bonding social capital is crucial during immediate crises, providing the emotional and practical support necessary to cope with adversity. Bridging social capital enables communities to pull together diverse resources and skills, promoting effective collective action. Linking social capital opens up access to external support and resources that might not otherwise be available, including governmental aid and private sector contributions.

Strengthening Community Ties

Enhancing social capital involves strengthening the relationships within a community. This can be achieved through community events, volunteer programs, and local organizations that bring people together around common interests and goals. Regular social interactions foster a sense of community and mutual understanding, which is essential for cooperation during times of crisis.

Community centers, sports leagues, cultural festivals, and local committees are all examples of initiatives that can build social capital. By encouraging participation in these activities, communities can enhance trust and reciprocity among their members, creating a stronger, more cohesive social fabric.

Promoting Trust and Reciprocity

Trust is a fundamental element of social capital. When community members trust each other and local institutions, they are more likely to cooperate and support mutual aid initiatives. Trust is built through consistent, positive interactions and experiences that demonstrate reliability and goodwill. Communities can foster trust by ensuring transparency in decision-making processes, promoting fair practices, and encouraging open communication.

Reciprocity strengthens social ties by establishing a culture where people feel obliged to help others who have helped them, creating a cycle of mutual assistance. This is particularly important in times of crisis, as it ensures that resources and support are distributed throughout the community.

Leveraging Social Networks in Crisis Response

In the event of a crisis, social capital can be a vital resource. Communities with strong social networks are better equipped to organize grassroots responses to disasters, distribute resources efficiently, and provide psychological support to those affected. For example, during natural disasters, neighbors often rely on each other for immediate assistance, such as sharing food and water, providing temporary shelter, and assisting with evacuation efforts.

Social workers and community leaders can harness these networks to coordinate more effective responses and ensure that information about aid and resources reaches all segments of the community. Furthermore, after the immediate crisis, social capital facilitates collaborative recovery efforts, helping to rebuild infrastructure, restore services, and support emotional recovery.

Social Capital and Long-Term Community Development

Beyond crisis management, social capital is crucial for long-term community development and resilience. Communities that enjoy strong social networks and high levels of trust are better able to engage in collective problem-solving, participate in civic activities, and influence local governance. These communities are often more successful in advocating for their needs and securing necessary resources for development projects.

Additionally, social capital can drive economic development by facilitating business connections and entrepreneurial initiatives. Networks of contacts can help budding entrepreneurs find mentors, secure funding, and access broader markets. This economic stimulation contributes to the overall resilience of the community by creating jobs, enhancing income stability, and diversifying the local economy.

Challenges and Strategies for Building Social Capital

Building social capital can be challenging, especially in diverse or transient communities where people may have fewer opportunities for repeated interactions. To overcome these challenges, strategies that specifically target community integration and inclusivity are needed. This might involve language and cultural sensitivity training, programs that celebrate diversity, and initiatives that specifically aim to integrate marginalized groups into the community.

By focusing on these strategies, communities can enhance their resilience through the development of social capital. This involves nurturing a culture of trust and reciprocity, engaging in activities that strengthen communal ties, leveraging social networks in times of need, and using these relationships to foster broader community development and economic growth. Social capital not only aids in recovery but also enhances the overall quality of life, making communities more cohesive, responsive, and resilient.

"*Every act of resilience is a story of triumph not just over adversity, but of the human spirit. These stories inspire, teach, and remind us of our inherent strength. They are beacons that guide us through our darkest hours.*"

ℭℬ

XI

Environmental Challenges and Community Resilience

Environmental challenges such as climate change, pollution, and natural disasters have profound impacts on communities, influencing not only their physical landscapes but also their social structures and economic stability. Building resilience against these challenges is crucial for ensuring that communities can anticipate, prepare for, respond to, and recover from environmental adversities. Resilience in this context involves both adaptation strategies to deal with the changes and mitigation efforts to prevent or reduce the severity of these environmental challenges.

Understanding the Impact of Environmental Issues

The effects of environmental challenges on communities are multifaceted. Climate change, for instance, leads to more frequent and severe weather events like hurricanes, floods, and droughts, which can devastate communities. These events disrupt lives, damage infrastructure, and can lead to significant economic losses. Additionally, slower onset changes such as rising sea levels and increased temperatures can alter agricultural productivity and water availability, impacting food security and livelihoods.

Pollution, another critical environmental issue, affects air, water, and soil quality, posing health risks to the population. For example, poor air quality can lead to respiratory problems and other health issues, reducing the quality of life and increasing healthcare costs. Contaminated water sources caused by industrial discharge or agricultural runoff can lead to waterborne diseases, further straining community health resources.

Strategies for Enhancing Environmental Resilience

Building resilience requires a proactive approach to both mitigate the causes of environmental degradation and adapt to its impacts. Here are several strategies that communities can employ:

1. Sustainable Resource Management

Effective management of natural resources is crucial for mitigating environmental impacts. This includes sustainable water management systems that conserve water and protect against droughts, as well as sustainable forestry and agriculture practices that increase land productivity and prevent degradation. Implementing these practices not only preserves the environment but also ensures that resources are available for future generations.

2. Disaster Preparedness and Response

Enhancing a community's preparedness for natural disasters is vital. This involves developing and implementing disaster response plans, improving infrastructure resilience, and educating the community about disaster preparedness. For example, flood-prone areas can benefit from improved drainage systems, raised buildings, and regular community drills. Additionally, establishing local emergency response teams and communication systems ensures that communities can quickly respond to and recover from disasters.

3. Community-Based Environmental Monitoring

Communities can engage in environmental monitoring to keep track of pollution levels, the status of wildlife, and other environmental indicators. This grassroots approach empowers community members, provides valuable data for decision-making, and fosters a greater connection to the local environment. For instance, community-based water quality testing can detect pollution sources early, allowing for quicker responses to prevent contamination.

4. Health Initiatives Related to Environmental Issues

Public health initiatives that address the health impacts of environmental issues are essential. This includes healthcare services that specialize in treating conditions caused by poor environmental conditions, such as respiratory problems from air pollution or illnesses from contaminated water. Health education campaigns can also raise awareness about the health risks associated with environmental degradation and promote behaviors that support environmental health.

5. Economic Diversification

Economic diversification is another key aspect of resilience. Communities that rely heavily on climate-sensitive sectors, such as agriculture or tourism, are particularly vulnerable to environmental changes. Diversifying the local economy to include less vulnerable sectors can reduce risk and improve community stability during environmental disruptions.

6. Advocacy and Policy Engagement

Community resilience can be significantly enhanced by engaging in advocacy and influencing policy. By advocating for stronger environmental protection laws, communities can drive systemic change that reduces the impact of environmental issues. Local communities can also work with government agencies to implement policies that promote renewable energy, reduce emissions, and protect natural habitats, contributing to both mitigation and adaptation efforts.

7. Building Social Capital

Strong social networks enhance community resilience by promoting cooperation and collective action in response to environmental challenges. When communities have a strong sense of unity and trust, they are better able to mobilize resources, share information, and support each other during crises.

Environmental challenges pose significant risks to communities, but through resilience-building strategies, these effects can be mitigated. Sustainable resource management, disaster preparedness, community-based monitoring, public health initiatives, economic diversification, advocacy, and strong social networks are all critical components of a resilient community. By implementing these strategies, communities can enhance their ability to withstand, adapt to, and recover from environmental challenges, ensuring their long-term sustainability and well-being.

"Building resilience is about recognizing the small victories as well as the monumental achievements. Each step forward, no matter how small, is a step toward a stronger community. It is the persistent efforts that forge the path to recovery."

༄

XII
Education for Resilience

Education plays a pivotal role in fostering resilience within communities. By equipping individuals with the necessary knowledge and skills, educational programs and initiatives can prepare community members to effectively respond to and recover from various challenges, be they social, economic, or environmental. Effective education for resilience transcends traditional learning environments, encompassing a wide array of formal and informal settings and tailored programs that address specific community needs.

Core Components of Resilience Education

Education for resilience focuses on developing critical thinking, problem-solving abilities, emotional intelligence, and practical skills that individuals need to thrive in the face of adversity. These programs often include elements of disaster preparedness, environmental stewardship, economic skills, and social responsibility. By integrating these components into educational curricula, communities can create a culture of preparedness and adaptive capacity.

Disaster Preparedness Education

Educational initiatives that focus on disaster preparedness are crucial for communities frequently exposed to natural disasters such as hurricanes, floods, earthquakes, or wildfires. These programs teach essential survival skills, emergency response techniques, and evacuation procedures. Schools, community centers, and local government institutions often facilitate such programs, ensuring that all demographic groups, including children, adults, and the elderly, understand how to react swiftly and safely during emergencies.

For example, schools may incorporate drills and simulation exercises into their regular activities, helping students and staff practice their response to various emergency scenarios. Community workshops can offer training on first aid, emergency communication systems, and the use of survival kits, enhancing the community's overall preparedness and resilience.

Environmental Education

Environmental education programs are vital in teaching community members about sustainable practices and the importance of environmental conservation. These programs can foster a greater appreciation for the local environment and educate individuals on how their actions can impact it. Topics might include water conservation, waste reduction, recycling processes, and the impacts of pollution.

Such education not only promotes environmental stewardship but also empowers individuals to make informed decisions that contribute to the sustainability and resilience of their communities. For instance, learning about sustainable agriculture can encourage farmers to adopt practices that maintain soil health and reduce vulnerability to droughts and floods.

Financial Literacy and Economic Education

Financial literacy programs are essential for economic resilience, providing community members with the skills needed to manage personal finances, understand economic risks, and seize opportunities for economic improvement. These programs cover budgeting, saving, investing, and understanding credit, which are critical for economic stability, especially in underserved or economically volatile communities.

Economic education can also include entrepreneurial training, which equips individuals with the skills to start and manage businesses. This type of education supports economic diversification and innovation within the community, contributing to its overall economic resilience.

Social and Emotional Learning (SEL)

Social and emotional learning (SEL) is a crucial aspect of resilience education, focusing on developing skills such as empathy, self-awareness, and emotional regulation. These programs help individuals navigate interpersonal and community relationships more effectively and respond to challenges with greater emotional intelligence.

SEL programs are often implemented in schools, but they are also beneficial in community settings, particularly in areas affected by social tensions or ongoing recovery from past traumas. By enhancing emotional resilience, communities can better manage social conflicts and support collective recovery efforts.

Lifelong Learning and Community Education Programs

Education for resilience should not be confined to formal schooling; it needs to be a lifelong pursuit. Adult education and community learning programs can play a significant role in continuously enhancing community resilience. These programs might include workshops on new technologies, lectures about global and local economic trends, or courses on health and wellness.

Community education centers and online platforms can provide flexible learning opportunities that cater to the diverse needs of the community. Such initiatives ensure that all members of the community have ongoing access to education that enhances their personal and collective resilience.

Integrating Technology in Resilience Education

Leveraging technology in education can significantly enhance the reach and effectiveness of resilience-building initiatives. Online learning platforms, virtual simulations, and interactive apps can provide scalable solutions for teaching resilience skills. For instance, virtual reality simulations of disaster scenarios can offer realistic training opportunities that are difficult to replicate in conventional educational settings.

Community Engagement and Participatory Learning

Engaging the community in the design and implementation of educational programs ensures that these initiatives are relevant and adapted to local needs. Participatory learning experiences, where community members contribute their knowledge and skills, can enhance the relevance and impact of the education provided.

By fostering a collaborative approach to education, communities can develop programs that are not only informative but also empowering. Engaging local experts, leaders, and stakeholders in educational efforts helps build a sense of ownership and responsibility towards community resilience.

Education for resilience is a comprehensive approach that encompasses a variety of programs and initiatives aimed at preparing individuals and communities to effectively face and overcome challenges. Through disaster preparedness, environmental education, financial literacy, social and emotional learning, lifelong learning opportunities, technology integration, and community engagement, educational programs can build a resilient foundation that supports sustainable development and enhances the quality of life for all community members.

"In the library of life's challenges, resilience is the
book we write together. Each chapter filled with
stories of courage, unity, and perseverance. Read it
closely, for it teaches us the lessons of strength and
renewal."

৪৩

XIII

Community-Led Initiatives

Community-led initiatives play a crucial role in enhancing local resilience by harnessing the collective strength, knowledge, and resources of community members. These projects not only address specific local challenges but also empower residents, foster social cohesion, and enhance the overall capacity of communities to manage future adversities. This comprehensive exploration highlights various successful community-led projects across diverse regions, demonstrating how grassroots efforts can effectively build resilience.

Urban Gardening and Greening Projects

One successful example of community-led initiatives involves urban gardening and greening projects. These initiatives typically aim to transform vacant or underutilized urban spaces into vibrant green areas or community gardens. For instance, the Detroit Urban Gardening Movement (DUGM) revitalized numerous abandoned lots throughout the city, converting them into productive gardens that now provide fresh produce to local residents. This not only improves food security but also enhances community cohesion as residents work together to manage these spaces. Additionally, these green spaces contribute to environmental sustainability by improving air quality and reducing urban heat island effects, thereby enhancing the community's resilience to environmental challenges.

Community Emergency Response Teams (CERTs)

Community Emergency Response Teams (CERTs) are another prime example of community-led resilience. These teams consist of volunteers trained to assist in disaster response efforts within their communities. For instance, in Japan, following the 2011 earthquake and tsunami, local CERTs played a crucial role in providing immediate assistance, from first aid to search and rescue operations before professional emergency services could arrive. By relying on local knowledge and the immediate availability of volunteers, CERTs can significantly reduce the impact of disasters on communities, proving that preparedness and local involvement are key to resilience.

Local Energy Cooperatives

Energy cooperatives are an innovative form of community-led initiative that strengthens resilience by promoting energy independence. In Germany, the village of Schönau pioneered a community-owned energy cooperative that produces and distributes renewable energy to the local population. This initiative began as a grassroots movement against nuclear power and has since evolved into a successful model for sustainable energy production, contributing to the community's economic stability and environmental resilience. The cooperative not only ensures a reliable and sustainable energy supply but also keeps energy revenues within the community, reinforcing economic resilience.

Water Management Initiatives

In many parts of the world, community-led water management initiatives have proven essential in addressing water scarcity and quality issues. An example of this can be found in Rajasthan, India, where local communities have revived traditional rainwater harvesting techniques to combat severe water shortages. The construction and restoration of 'johads'—small earthen check dams—have been crucial in recharging groundwater levels, ensuring water availability throughout the year. This not only supports agriculture and daily needs but also prevents water conflicts, showcasing how traditional knowledge and community action can lead to sustainable water management solutions.

Community-Based Tourism

Community-based tourism initiatives empower local communities by allowing them to manage and benefit from tourism activities directly. Such projects often focus on preserving local cultures and environments while providing economic opportunities. In Costa Rica, several indigenous communities have developed tourism projects that showcase their cultural heritage and natural surroundings. These initiatives not only provide a sustainable income source but also foster a sense of pride and cultural preservation, enhancing social resilience against the pressures of globalization and external economic fluctuations.

Neighborhood Watch Programs

Neighborhood watch programs, often initiated by residents to reduce local crime rates, also enhance community resilience by improving public safety and fostering a sense of community. Participants in these programs collaborate with local law enforcement to monitor neighborhood activities, share information, and implement safety measures. This collective vigilance not only deters crime but also strengthens community bonds as residents unite for a common cause, building trust and mutual support that are essential in times of crisis.

Digital Platforms for Community Engagement

In the digital age, online platforms have become powerful tools for community-led initiatives. For example, in New York City, the "Nextdoor" app allows neighbors to share information, goods, and services, and to mobilize resources quickly in response to local needs such as food drives, blood donations, or emergency responses. This digital engagement enhances community resilience by maintaining a constant flow of communication and support among residents, proving that technology can be a significant enabler of community cohesion and mutual aid.

These diverse examples of community-led initiatives demonstrate the vast potential of grassroots efforts in building local resilience. Whether through environmental projects, emergency preparedness, sustainable economic activities, or innovative use of technology, these initiatives highlight the importance of community involvement in addressing local challenges. By empowering residents to take charge of their community's well-being, these projects not only address immediate needs but also lay the groundwork for long-term sustainability and resilience, ensuring that communities are better equipped to face future challenges together.

"The fabric of resilience is stitched together with the threads of mutual support and collective courage. When the fabric is tested by crises, it holds strong, protecting and preserving the community. This is the true power of unity."

൙

XIV

Collaborations and Partnerships

Collaborations and partnerships across different sectors are crucial in enhancing the effectiveness of resilience initiatives. By bringing together diverse stakeholders, including governments, businesses, non-profits, and community groups, these partnerships leverage a broader range of resources, expertise, and influence, creating more comprehensive and sustainable solutions to challenges facing communities. This integrated approach is particularly vital in addressing complex issues such as disaster preparedness, economic recovery, environmental conservation, and social cohesion, all of which are essential components of community resilience.

The Role of Cross-Sector Partnerships

Cross-sector partnerships enhance resilience by facilitating a holistic approach to problem-solving that no single sector could achieve alone. These collaborations are designed to bridge gaps between different areas of expertise and resources, ensuring that initiatives are well-rounded and address multiple aspects of resilience simultaneously.

1. Leveraging Diverse Resources

One of the primary benefits of cross-sector partnerships is the ability to pool and leverage resources from various sources. For example, a partnership between local government, private businesses, and non-profit organizations can bring together funding, materials, and human resources that would be beyond the reach of any partner operating independently. This is particularly important in resource-intensive endeavors like building infrastructure to withstand natural disasters or launching large-scale economic development projects.

2. Enhancing Expertise and Knowledge Sharing

Cross-sector partnerships also facilitate the sharing of knowledge and expertise among partners, which can lead to more innovative and effective solutions. Each sector brings unique strengths and perspectives to the table. For instance, while government agencies can provide regulatory support and public funding, private companies might bring in cutting-edge technology and management expertise, and non-profits can offer deep community insights and flexible, on-the-ground engagement strategies.

3. Improving Program Reach and Impact

By combining forces, organizations within a partnership can expand the reach and impact of their initiatives. This is particularly effective in large-scale public health campaigns or community education programs, where the combined networks of multiple organizations can disseminate information more widely and effectively than any single organization could alone. For example, a public-private partnership aimed at improving health education might combine the logistical capabilities of a government, the outreach platforms of a media company, and the community access of a network of non-profit organizations.

4. Fostering Innovation Through Diverse Inputs

The diverse perspectives present within cross-sector partnerships can stimulate innovation, leading to novel solutions that address complex community challenges. When different sectors collaborate, the creative constraints of one sector can be offset by the capabilities of another, potentially leading to breakthroughs in how services are delivered or problems are solved. For example, tech companies can work with environmental groups and municipal governments to develop smart-city technologies that improve energy efficiency, waste management, and water conservation.

5. Building Trust and Social Capital

Cross-sector partnerships can help build trust and social capital both within and between communities and sectors. When various sectors work together and achieve positive outcomes, it reinforces trust in institutions and among community members. This social capital is invaluable, particularly in times of crisis, as it facilitates quicker and more cooperative community responses.

6. Sustaining Initiatives Over Time

The involvement of multiple sectors can also lend greater sustainability to resilience initiatives. By involving a variety of stakeholders, these partnerships ensure that projects have the support needed to continue beyond the lifecycle of single funding cycles or election terms. This is crucial for long-term initiatives, such as those aimed at climate change adaptation or sustained economic development.

Successful Examples of Cross-Sector Partnerships

Numerous examples highlight the success of cross-sector partnerships in building community resilience. For instance, after Hurricane Katrina, a famous partnership between local governments, federal agencies, non-profits, and private businesses played a critical role in rebuilding and strengthening the resilience of New Orleans. These partnerships helped to restore critical infrastructure, provide housing, and support economic recovery, showcasing how collaborative efforts can rebuild a community more effectively than isolated actions.

In another example, international partnerships such as those between global health organizations, governments, and pharmaceutical companies have been crucial in responding to global health crises, such as the COVID-19 pandemic. These partnerships facilitated the rapid development and distribution of vaccines and coordinated public health responses across borders, demonstrating the power of collaborative action in facing global challenges.

Challenges in Cross-Sector Partnerships

Despite their benefits, forming and maintaining effective cross-sector partnerships can be challenging. Issues such as differing goals, misaligned incentives, and variations in operational cultures can impede collaboration. To overcome these challenges, clear communication, shared goals, mutually beneficial arrangements, and strong leadership are essential. Establishing formal agreements on roles and responsibilities, as well as continuous monitoring and evaluation, can also help sustain these partnerships.

In conclusion, cross-sector partnerships are indispensable in enhancing community resilience. By pooling resources, sharing knowledge, expanding reach, and fostering innovation, these collaborations bring comprehensive solutions to complex challenges. As communities worldwide face increasing threats from environmental changes, economic shifts, and social disparities, the importance of such partnerships will only continue to grow, underlining the need for sustained, collaborative approaches to building a resilient future.

"Resilience is not a trait of the individual but a
feature of the community. It flourishes where there
is mutual aid, where there is teamwork. It is the
collective power to face any adversity with
unwavering courage."

☙

XV

Technology and Innovation

Technology and innovation have become increasingly central to social work, offering new tools and approaches that enhance the effectiveness of services and expand the reach of support systems. These advancements are particularly significant in the context of community resilience, where they can improve the delivery of social services, facilitate better data management, enhance communication and engagement, and ultimately lead to more proactive and informed interventions.

Innovative Technologies in Social Work

Digital and Mobile Technologies: Mobile applications and online platforms have revolutionized the way social services are delivered. Apps can provide immediate access to crisis intervention services, mental health support, and resources for dealing with domestic violence or homelessness. For example, mobile apps like SafeNight provide a way for domestic violence survivors to find immediate shelter. Additionally, mobile technology facilitates greater accessibility to services, particularly for people in remote or underserved areas who may not have easy access to traditional in-person counseling or support services.

Telehealth Services: Telehealth has been a transformative force in social work, particularly in the areas of mental health and counseling. It allows social workers to provide consultation and therapy sessions via video calls, significantly expanding the reach of these services. This is especially beneficial in rural or isolated communities, where specialist mental health services might not be physically available. During the COVID-19 pandemic, telehealth proved essential in continuing mental health services without the risk of virus transmission.

Big Data and Analytics: Big data technologies allow social workers and community planners to understand and predict community needs better. By analyzing large sets of data from various sources, social workers can identify trends and risk factors associated with social issues such as poverty, crime, and health disparities. This predictive capability is crucial for deploying resources more effectively and for intervening before issues escalate into more serious problems.

Geographic Information Systems (GIS): GIS technology is used in social work to map social services, community resources, demographic trends, and areas of need. This can help in planning the distribution of resources and in identifying underserved areas. GIS can also play a vital role in disaster response and planning, allowing social workers to quickly identify which areas are most affected by a crisis and need urgent assistance.

Blockchain Technology: Although still in its early stages of adoption in social work, blockchain offers potential for enhancing the transparency, security, and efficiency of social services. For example, blockchain can be used to create secure and immutable records for child welfare, reducing the risk of data breaches and improving data sharing among authorized professionals.

Innovative Practices in Social Work

Integrated Service Delivery: Innovative service delivery models such as integrated social services are transforming social work. These models involve the coordination of various social services such as healthcare, housing, and education to provide a holistic approach to supporting individuals and families. This integration can be facilitated by technology platforms that allow different service providers to access and share information seamlessly.

Community Participation Platforms: Online platforms and social media have enabled greater community involvement in social work processes. These platforms allow communities to voice their concerns, participate in decision-making processes, and collaborate in resilience-building activities. They also facilitate more transparent communication between service providers and community members, building trust and ensuring that services are aligned with community needs.

E-therapy and Online Support Groups: The rise of online therapeutic services and support groups has made mental health support more accessible. These services provide flexibility for clients and can be particularly helpful for those who might feel stigmatized by seeking face-to-face counseling. They also allow for the creation of specialized support groups that might not be viable in a local setting due to limited numbers of participants with similar issues.

Virtual Reality (VR) and Augmented Reality (AR): VR and AR are being explored for their potential in training social workers and in therapeutic settings. For example, VR can simulate real-life scenarios for social work students, preparing them for fieldwork in a controlled environment. AR can be used in therapeutic settings to help clients overcome phobias or to simulate social situations for individuals with social anxiety.

Challenges and Considerations

While technology and innovation offer significant benefits, they also come with challenges. Issues such as digital divide, privacy concerns, and the need for proper training can hinder the effective implementation of technology in social work. Ensuring equitable access to technological solutions is crucial, as is protecting sensitive client data. Additionally, while technology can enhance service delivery, it should not replace the human element that is fundamental to social work.

Technology and innovative practices are profoundly transforming social work, enhancing the ability of professionals to support and build resilience within communities. These technologies enable more informed decision-making, wider service reach, and more efficient resource allocation, contributing significantly to the effectiveness of social work interventions. However, the integration of these technologies must be handled with care to ensure they complement traditional social work practices and maintain the essential human touch that underpins the profession.

"As social workers lay the bricks of resilience, each brick is infused with hope and care. With every layer, they build up the community's strength to face future storms. This construction is not just of buildings, but of spirits and futures."

৪৩

XVI

Legal and Policy Frameworks for Resilience

Legal and policy frameworks play a crucial role in shaping the resilience of communities. They can either provide a strong foundation that supports and enhances resilience efforts or serve as barriers that hinder effective action. Understanding how these frameworks influence resilience is essential for policymakers, legal experts, and community leaders working to create more sustainable and adaptable communities.

Supportive Legal and Policy Environments

Comprehensive Disaster Management Laws: Effective disaster management laws are critical for enhancing community resilience. These laws typically provide guidelines for disaster preparedness, response, recovery, and mitigation. For instance, policies that mandate the construction of buildings to certain safety standards can significantly reduce the damage caused by natural disasters such as earthquakes and hurricanes.

Environmental Protection Regulations: Strong environmental policies are vital for preserving ecosystems that can buffer against environmental shocks. Regulations that limit pollution, manage natural resources sustainably, and protect critical habitats help maintain the environmental health of a community, which is a key aspect of its overall resilience.

Social Protection Policies: Legal frameworks that ensure a safety net for the most vulnerable populations contribute significantly to community resilience. These include policies related to healthcare, unemployment benefits, and social housing. For example, universal healthcare laws can prevent a health crisis from becoming a full-blown community disaster by ensuring that all citizens receive necessary medical care, regardless of their financial situation.

Economic Diversification and Support Laws: Policies that promote economic resilience through diversification and support for small and medium enterprises (SMEs) are crucial. These might include tax incentives for start-ups, grants for businesses in critical sectors, or laws that encourage foreign investment in diverse industries.

Education and Training Regulations: Laws that govern education and training systems can also impact community resilience. Policies that promote lifelong learning, vocational training, and re-skilling can help communities adapt to economic changes and technological advancements, ensuring a more resilient workforce.

Barriers to Resilience in Legal and Policy Frameworks

Inadequate Infrastructure Standards: Legal frameworks that fail to enforce stringent building codes or environmental regulations can leave communities vulnerable to disasters. In regions where such standards are lax or not adequately enforced, the damage from natural disasters can be significantly exacerbated, undermining the community's ability to respond and recover.

Short-term Planning Horizons: Policies that focus on immediate gains without consideration for long-term sustainability can hinder resilience. For example, urban development policies that prioritize rapid growth over sustainable planning may lead to inadequate infrastructure, environmental degradation, and increased vulnerability to urban flooding.

Lack of Integrated Policy Approaches: When policies are developed in silos without consideration for how different sectors interact, they can reduce the effectiveness of resilience efforts. For instance, water management policies that do not align with agricultural policies may lead to inefficiencies and conflicts that undermine the resilience of the food supply system.

Underfunded Social Programs: Legal frameworks that do not secure sufficient funding for social programs can create gaps in the social safety net. This underfunding can leave vulnerable populations without necessary support during and after crises, thereby weakening the overall resilience of the community.

Restrictive Policies on Community Engagement: Legal and policy frameworks that restrict civic engagement and community organizing can stifle grassroots resilience initiatives. Policies that limit public demonstrations, censor community activists, or constrain non-profit organizations can prevent communities from mobilizing effectively to address local challenges.

Enhancing Legal and Policy Frameworks for Resilience

To enhance community resilience, policymakers need to focus on creating integrated, well-funded, and forward-thinking legal and policy frameworks. This involves:

Ensuring that laws and policies are based on a thorough understanding of the local context and risks.

Engaging a wide range of stakeholders in the policymaking process to capture diverse perspectives and ensure that policies are comprehensive and inclusive.

Regularly reviewing and updating policies and laws to adapt to changing environmental, social, and economic conditions.

Investing in public awareness and education to ensure that communities understand and can effectively engage with resilience policies.

Developing mechanisms for rapid policy adjustment in response to disasters or unexpected challenges, enabling more flexible and adaptive governance.

Legal and policy environments are foundational to community resilience. By carefully crafting laws and policies that support comprehensive disaster management, environmental protection, social protection, economic stability, and community engagement, governments can significantly enhance the capacity of communities to withstand and recover from adversities. Conversely, recognizing and reforming policies that serve as barriers to resilience is equally important in ensuring that communities are not only prepared for today's challenges but are also adaptable to tomorrow's uncertainties.

"Community resilience is like a river that flows strong and steady, fed by the streams of individual efforts and collective actions. It carves pathways through the toughest terrains, always moving forward, always enduring. Such is the power of united flows."

ॐ

XVII

Cultural Competence in Social Work

Cultural competence in social work is essential for effectively addressing the diverse needs of communities. This practice entails understanding, respecting, and appropriately responding to the cultural differences that significantly influence clients' perceptions, behaviors, and interactions within their social environments. Social workers equipped with cultural competence can provide more effective and personalized services that respect their clients' cultural backgrounds, which is crucial in fostering trust and improving service outcomes.

Understanding Cultural Competence

Cultural competence involves more than just awareness of cultural differences; it requires social workers to engage actively with these differences to enhance their interactions and interventions. This includes knowledge of clients' cultural practices, beliefs, values, and experiences, as well as an understanding of how these cultural factors influence clients' responses to social problems, social services, and interventions. Cultural competence also extends to organizational practices and policies that social workers must navigate to advocate effectively for their clients.

The Impact of Culture on Social Work

Culture deeply impacts how individuals perceive and deal with issues such as mental health, family relationships, education, and employment. For example, in some cultures, mental health issues might be stigmatized, which can affect individuals' willingness to seek help. In family dynamics, beliefs about roles and responsibilities can vary significantly between cultures and affect how family interventions should be approached. Recognizing these cultural influences is vital for social workers to provide relevant and respectful support.

Strategies for Building Cultural Competence

Education and Training: Ongoing education and training in cultural competence are crucial for social workers. This should include both formal education, such as courses and workshops, and informal learning opportunities, such as community immersion and interaction with diverse groups. Training programs should cover specific cultural knowledge as well as general skills in cultural sensitivity and communication.

Self-Awareness: Social workers must continually assess and understand their cultural biases and the way these biases might affect their practice. Self-awareness activities can help social workers recognize their assumptions and prejudices, ensuring that these do not interfere with their professionalism and effectiveness.

Client-Centered Communication: Effective communication is a cornerstone of cultural competence. Social workers should use language that is accessible and respectful, avoiding jargon or colloquialisms that might not translate across cultures. They should also be adept at non-verbal communication cues, which can vary significantly between cultures.

Community Engagement: Engaging with the communities in which social workers practice is essential for building cultural competence. This engagement helps social workers gain deeper insights into the cultural norms and values of the populations they serve. It can involve participating in community events, forming partnerships with local leaders, and respecting community hierarchies and structures.

Incorporating Cultural Practices in Interventions: Where appropriate, integrating cultural practices and values into social work interventions can enhance their acceptance and effectiveness. This might involve incorporating traditional practices into mental health therapy or acknowledging and respecting cultural rituals in family counseling.

Advocacy for Culturally Competent Policies: Social workers also play a role in advocating for policies that recognize and respect cultural diversity within communities. This can involve pushing for service delivery models that are culturally adaptive and for the inclusion of community members in policy development processes.

Benefits of Cultural Competence in Social Work

The benefits of cultural competence in social work are extensive:

Improved Service Delivery: Culturally competent social workers are more likely to develop effective, personalized intervention strategies that account for clients' cultural backgrounds.

Enhanced Client Trust and Engagement: When clients feel understood and respected, they are more likely to engage actively in social work processes and interventions.

Better Outcomes: By tailoring services and interventions to the cultural contexts of clients, social workers can achieve better outcomes, whether in mental health, family dynamics, education, or other areas.

Increased Professional Effectiveness: Cultural competence can enhance a social worker's overall effectiveness by expanding their understanding and skills in dealing with diverse populations.

Challenges in Implementing Cultural Competence

Despite its importance, implementing cultural competence can face several challenges, including resistance to change, limited resources for training, and difficulties in assessing cultural needs accurately. Overcoming these challenges requires organizational commitment, adequate funding, and continuous professional development.

Cultural competence is a fundamental aspect of modern social work. It enables social workers to effectively address the diverse needs of the communities they serve by fostering understanding, respect, and appropriate responses to cultural differences. As societies continue to become more diverse, the need for cultural competence in social work will only grow, making it an essential skill for social workers aiming to provide effective, equitable, and respectful services.

"In the heart of resilience lies the spirit of
adaptation—the ability to transform challenges
into opportunities. It is a dynamic dance of
learning, growing, and evolving. With each step, the
community moves closer to a future unbounded by
the fears of yesterday."

ॐ

XVIII

Monitoring and Evaluation of Resilience

Monitoring and evaluation (M&E) are critical components of any resilience-building project, providing essential feedback that can inform decision-making and improve project outcomes. Effective M&E helps project teams understand whether resilience initiatives are achieving their intended impacts, where adjustments may be needed, and how future projects can be optimized for better success. Developing a comprehensive M&E strategy for resilience projects involves several key steps and considerations.

Setting Clear Objectives and Indicators

The first step in effective M&E is to clearly define the objectives of the resilience-building project. These objectives should be specific, measurable, achievable, relevant, and time-bound (SMART). Once objectives are set, appropriate indicators must be developed to measure progress towards these objectives. Indicators should be directly linked to the outcomes the project intends to influence and should be measurable through available methods and resources.

For resilience projects, indicators might include measures of increased community awareness and preparedness, improvements in infrastructure stability, or enhanced economic diversification. Environmental resilience projects might measure changes in local biodiversity or reductions in pollution levels.

Baseline Data Collection

Before implementing a resilience project, it is essential to collect baseline data. This data serves as a reference point against which changes can be measured throughout the project's lifecycle. Baseline data should be comprehensive, covering all aspects that the project will influence. For instance, if a project aims to enhance economic resilience by supporting local businesses, baseline data on local business performance, employment rates, and economic output would be necessary.

Continuous Monitoring

Monitoring involves the regular collection and analysis of data to assess progress against expected outcomes. It provides ongoing insights into the effectiveness of the project and can help identify any deviations from the plan early in the process. Effective monitoring relies on consistent data collection methods and regular reporting from all stakeholders involved.

For example, a project aimed at increasing community preparedness for natural disasters might involve regular surveys of residents' knowledge and preparedness levels, along with assessments of community response capabilities during drills or actual events.

Periodic and Final Evaluations

Evaluation assesses the effectiveness and impact of a project at specific points in time – typically mid-term and at the end of the project. Unlike continuous monitoring, evaluation aims to provide an in-depth analysis of why certain outcomes were or were not achieved and whether the overall impact aligns with the project's objectives.

Evaluations should answer questions such as:

Did the project achieve its intended outcomes?

What were the major factors influencing the success or failure of the project?

How effectively were resources utilized?

What lessons have been learned, and how can they inform future projects?

Feedback Mechanisms and Stakeholder Engagement

Effective M&E systems incorporate feedback mechanisms that allow stakeholders, including community members, to provide input on project processes and outcomes. This feedback is crucial for maintaining the relevance and responsiveness of the project. Engaging stakeholders not only enhances the quality of the data collected but also ensures that the project remains aligned with community needs and expectations.

Data Management and Utilization

Managing the data collected through monitoring and evaluation activities is a critical task that requires careful planning. Data should be stored securely, organized systematically, and analyzed competently to extract meaningful insights. The utilization of this data is just as important as its collection. Insights gained from M&E activities should be actively used to adjust project strategies, improve implementation practices, and inform policy-making.

Capacity Building for M&E

Building capacity for effective monitoring and evaluation is essential, particularly in community-led projects where local stakeholders may not have formal training in M&E techniques. Training sessions, workshops, and ongoing support for local teams can enhance their ability to conduct reliable and useful M&E.

Adaptation and Learning

Finally, an effective M&E strategy is adaptive. It should allow for modifications in the monitoring and evaluation plans as the project progresses and as new challenges and opportunities arise. This adaptability is key to maintaining the relevance and effectiveness of resilience projects in dynamic environments.

Monitoring and evaluation are essential for ensuring that resilience-building projects meet their goals and contribute positively to community resilience. By establishing clear objectives and indicators, collecting baseline data, implementing robust monitoring, conducting thorough evaluations, and engaging stakeholders throughout the process, project teams can not only measure the impacts of their efforts but also learn from their experiences to continuously improve resilience initiatives.

"The echoes of resilience are heard in the voices of those who have faced the storms and emerged stronger. These voices form a chorus of hope and determination that inspires others to rise. Let us listen and learn, for these stories light our way."

ॐ

XIX

Challenges and Barriers to Building Resilience

Building resilience in communities is a complex process, fraught with various challenges and barriers that can hinder effective implementation and sustainability of resilience efforts. These challenges can be environmental, social, economic, and institutional in nature, and they often require comprehensive strategies to overcome. Understanding these challenges is crucial for social workers, community leaders, and policymakers to develop more effective resilience-building initiatives.

1. Resource Constraints

One of the most significant barriers to building resilience is the lack of resources. Many communities, especially those in low-income or developing regions, face severe limitations in financial, human, and technological resources. This scarcity can impede the ability to implement essential infrastructure projects, social programs, and emergency preparedness measures. For social workers, resource constraints often mean they cannot provide services to all who need them, or they must do so with inadequate tools and support.

2. Institutional and Policy Limitations

Institutional barriers also play a crucial role in shaping resilience efforts. These can include bureaucratic red tape, inflexible policies, and fragmented or siloed government structures that impede coordinated and swift action. For example, when different government agencies do not collaborate effectively, it can lead to inefficient use of resources and delays in response to crises. Furthermore, outdated or rigid regulations may not account for modern challenges and solutions, stifling innovation in resilience practices.

3. Social and Cultural Barriers

Social and cultural factors can also pose significant barriers to resilience. In many communities, social norms and cultural practices may prevent certain groups from participating fully in resilience-building activities. For instance, in some cultures, women may not be allowed to participate in decision-making processes, which can hinder efforts that would benefit from their insight and involvement. Additionally, resistance to change is a common cultural barrier that social workers often encounter, as individuals and groups may be reluctant to adopt new practices or technologies.

4. Lack of Awareness and Education

A lack of awareness and education about resilience and related issues can impede community efforts to prepare for and respond to challenges. Without a proper understanding of the risks they face and the strategies that can mitigate these risks, community members may not be motivated to engage in resilience-building activities. Social workers often need to spend considerable time and resources educating communities, which can delay other resilience efforts.

5. Environmental Degradation and Climate Change

Environmental challenges such as climate change and ecological degradation pose significant barriers to community resilience. These issues can exacerbate the frequency and severity of natural disasters, strain natural resources, and lead to health problems that burden communities and social systems. Addressing these challenges often requires large-scale interventions that can be beyond the scope and capacity of individual communities and social workers.

6. Economic Challenges

Economic instability is another major barrier to building resilience. Economic downturns, unemployment, and poverty can all undermine resilience efforts by limiting community resources and increasing vulnerability to disasters and other crises. For social workers, economic barriers may manifest as increased demand for social services at a time when funding and resources are dwindling.

7. Political Instability and Conflict

In regions experiencing political instability or conflict, building resilience can be particularly challenging. Such conditions can disrupt social services, lead to the displacement of populations, and reduce the focus on long-term resilience strategies. For social workers, operating in these environments is not only challenging but can also be dangerous.

8. Technological Barriers

While technology can enhance resilience efforts, technological barriers such as lack of access to appropriate technology or insufficient skills to use it effectively can hinder these efforts. This is particularly true in less developed or rural areas where technological infrastructure may be lacking or where there is limited knowledge about how to leverage technology in resilience building.

9. Coordination and Communication Challenges

Effective coordination and communication among stakeholders are critical in resilience efforts. However, poor communication, misalignment of goals, and lack of collaborative frameworks can all serve as barriers. These challenges can lead to duplicated efforts, gaps in service delivery, and inefficiencies that detract from the overall goal of enhancing community resilience.

10. Psychological Barriers

Finally, psychological barriers such as fear, denial, and mental health struggles can impede individual and community willingness to engage in resilience-building. Understanding and addressing these psychological components are crucial for social workers, as they often need to support individuals in overcoming these barriers to participate effectively in resilience initiatives.

Overcoming these challenges requires a multifaceted approach involving strategic planning, resource allocation, education, and community engagement. By recognizing and addressing these barriers, communities, aided by social workers and other stakeholders, can develop more effective and sustainable strategies to build resilience and enhance their capacity to face future challenges.

☙

"Resilience is painted on the canvas of community with the brushstrokes of perseverance and dedication. Each stroke adds color and depth, illustrating the strength found in unity. This masterpiece reveals the beauty of collective resilience."

৪১

XX

Future Directions in Community Resilience

As communities worldwide continue to face a diverse range of challenges—from climate change and natural disasters to social and economic upheavals—the concept of resilience remains a pivotal focus of community development. The future of community resilience lies in adopting innovative approaches, leveraging new technologies, and fostering inclusive and sustainable practices that address the root causes of vulnerability. Social workers, pivotal in orchestrating these resilience-building efforts, must adapt and evolve to meet the changing needs of the communities they serve. This involves embracing new skills, tools, and collaborative strategies.

1. Embracing Technology and Digital Tools

One of the most significant trends in community resilience is the increased use of technology. Digital tools and data analytics are expected to play a crucial role in enhancing the ability of communities to predict, prepare for, and respond to crises. For social workers, this means becoming proficient in digital literacy, understanding how to utilize data effectively, and applying technology in innovative ways to improve service delivery. For instance, geographic information systems (GIS) can be used for mapping community resources and vulnerabilities, while mobile apps can facilitate real-time communication during emergencies.

2. Integrating Climate Resilience

As climate change continues to impact communities, integrating climate resilience into all aspects of planning and development will become increasingly important. This includes designing infrastructure and services that can withstand extreme weather events and transitioning to sustainable practices that reduce environmental impact. Social workers will need to advocate for policies that prioritize sustainability and work with communities to implement adaptation strategies that address both immediate and long-term environmental challenges.

3. Focusing on Mental Health and Psychosocial Support

The future of community resilience will also see a greater emphasis on mental health and psychosocial support. The increasing recognition of the psychological impacts of disasters and crises means that social workers will need to be equipped with skills to provide effective mental health care. This includes training in trauma-informed care, crisis intervention techniques, and community-based psychosocial support programs that promote long-term recovery and well-being.

4. Enhancing Social Equity

Addressing social inequities is fundamental to building resilient communities. Future resilience efforts will likely focus more on creating inclusive environments that ensure equitable access to resources and opportunities for all community members, particularly vulnerable populations. Social workers will play a key role in advocating for and implementing policies and programs that address inequality and foster social inclusion and justice.

5. Promoting Community-Led Initiatives

There is a growing trend towards empowering communities to lead their resilience-building efforts. This approach recognizes the value of local knowledge and the importance of community ownership in the success of resilience initiatives. Social workers can facilitate this process by supporting community leadership development, providing training and resources, and fostering partnerships that enhance community capacity to manage their own resilience projects.

6. Strengthening Multi-Sector Partnerships

Collaborations across different sectors—public, private, and non-profit—will be crucial for effective resilience-building. These partnerships can leverage diverse resources, expertise, and networks to address complex challenges more comprehensively. Social workers will need to develop skills in partnership development, negotiation, and collaborative project management to facilitate these multi-sector alliances effectively.

7. Advancing Policy Advocacy

Policy advocacy remains a critical component of future resilience efforts. Social workers will need to engage more actively in policy formulation and advocacy to ensure that resilience policies are comprehensive, evidence-based, and aligned with community needs. This includes advocating for funding, legislation, and regulations that support resilience-building across various domains, from health and housing to education and employment.

8. Continuous Learning and Adaptation

Finally, the field of community resilience is continually evolving, and social workers must commit to lifelong learning and professional development to stay current with new theories, practices, and technologies. This might involve participating in ongoing education and training programs, attending professional conferences, and staying engaged with the latest research and trends in resilience and social work practice.

The future of community resilience is dynamic and requires a proactive and adaptive approach from social workers. By embracing new technologies, integrating climate resilience, focusing on mental health support, enhancing social equity, promoting community-led initiatives, strengthening multi-sector partnerships, advancing policy advocacy, and committing to continuous learning, social workers can play a pivotal role in guiding communities towards a more resilient and sustainable future.

"Every community has the seeds of resilience, but it takes the hands of dedicated social workers and leaders to tend them. As they water these seeds with efforts and care, they grow into strong trees that stand tall against adversity. This is the garden where future generations will find shelter and strength."

XXI
SUMMARY

The journey through the multifaceted landscape of community resilience has provided us with an expansive view of the challenges, strategies, and innovations that define our efforts to build stronger, more adaptive communities. This summary seeks to encapsulate the essence and key insights from each chapter, highlighting the critical role of social work, community involvement, technology, and policy in fostering resilience across diverse settings.

Understanding and Enhancing Community Resilience

Community resilience is fundamentally about the capacity of communities to withstand, adapt to, and recover from adversities. This requires a robust understanding of what resilience entails—a dynamic process that integrates the community's physical, social, economic, and environmental aspects. We explored how communities could assess their resilience through various tools, focusing on both the vulnerabilities and strengths that define their current state.

The Role of Social Workers

Social workers play a pivotal role in resilience efforts. They act as connectors, educators, and advocates within communities, addressing immediate needs while fostering long-term resilience strategies. Their work involves not only crisis management but also proactive community planning and support, emphasizing the importance of preparedness and adaptive capacities in everyday social work practices.

Community-Led Initiatives and Partnerships

The effectiveness of resilience strategies is significantly enhanced by community-led initiatives and cross-sector partnerships. These approaches ensure that resilience-building efforts are inclusive and comprehensive, integrating the knowledge and resources of various stakeholders. Examples from around the world have shown that when communities lead their development, the results are more sustainable and better aligned with local needs and values.

Leveraging Technology and Innovation

Innovation and technology have transformed potential strategies for building community resilience. From digital platforms that facilitate better disaster response to applications that offer real-time data for crisis management, technology offers new pathways for enhancing community preparedness and response capabilities. Moreover, these tools can help bridge gaps in service delivery, particularly in underserved or remote areas, by providing critical information and connecting individuals with resources.

Cultural Competence and Inclusivity

Recognizing and respecting cultural diversity within communities is crucial for effective resilience-building. Cultural competence in social work ensures that services and interventions are appropriately tailored to the community's cultural context, enhancing their effectiveness and acceptance. This inclusivity is vital for fostering a sense of community ownership and participation in resilience initiatives.

Policy Frameworks and Legal Considerations

Legal and policy frameworks provide the structure within which community resilience efforts operate. Effective policies support resilience by enabling access to necessary resources, guiding the development of infrastructure, and ensuring that social systems are equipped to handle the demands of disaster response and recovery. Conversely, restrictive or outdated policies can significantly hinder these efforts, underscoring the need for ongoing advocacy and policy reform.

Education and Capacity Building

Education is a cornerstone of resilience, equipping individuals with the knowledge and skills necessary to navigate and manage crises. Resilience education spans formal school curriculums to community workshops, encompassing disaster preparedness, environmental stewardship, and financial literacy. This educational outreach is critical for cultivating a culture of resilience that permeates all levels of the community.

Addressing Barriers to Resilience

Building resilience is not without its challenges. Communities often face barriers such as resource limitations, bureaucratic hurdles, cultural resistance, and economic constraints. Overcoming these obstacles requires creative problem-solving, community mobilization, and the strategic allocation of resources to ensure that resilience-building efforts are both effective and equitable.

Future Directions in Community Resilience

Looking ahead, the field of community resilience is poised for significant evolution. Anticipated trends include increased emphasis on sustainable practices, enhanced integration of technology in disaster management and social services, and greater focus on mental health and psychosocial support as integral components of resilience. Moreover, the role of social workers will continue to expand as they adapt to these new challenges and opportunities, ensuring that communities not only survive but thrive in the face of adversity.

Building resilient communities is a complex, dynamic process that requires a multifaceted approach. By understanding the foundational elements of resilience, leveraging the power of community engagement, embracing technological advancements, and advocating for supportive policies, we can enhance the capacity of communities worldwide to navigate the uncertainties of the future with strength and confidence. This holistic approach to resilience not only prepares communities for specific challenges but also empowers them to create sustainable, thriving futures for generations to come.

CITATION AND REFERENCE

This book represents the culmination of extensive research and meticulous analysis, incorporating a diverse range of sources, including numerous books, scholarly studies, and personal experiences. Additionally, I have scoured various websites to gather relevant information and data essential for the compilation of this work. I have taken every precaution to ensure the accuracy of the information presented and have diligently cited all sources to acknowledge their contributions.

Despite these efforts, the possibility of inadvertent errors remains. I deeply value the insights of my readers and appreciate any feedback that can help identify and rectify such inaccuracies. I encourage you to bring any discrepancies to my attention.

Your feedback is not only welcome but crucial, as it will aid in correcting current editions and enhancing the content of future ones. I am committed to maintaining the highest standards of accuracy and reliability in my work and thank you for your support and understanding.

Additionally, I firmly uphold the principle of freedom of speech and expression as guaranteed under Article 19(1)(a) of the Constitution of India, and I respect the diverse viewpoints and expressions of all readers.

Other Books Of The Author

1. Empowering Minds: A Journey into Women's Self-Discovery and Power
2. The Dynamics of Motivation: Catalyzing Thought into Action
3. Meditation and Mental Well Being: The Path to Inner Peace and Clarity
4. The Psychology of Child Education: Nurturing Future Generations
5. Ethical Enlightenment: A Modern Guide to Living with Integrity
6. Voices of Empowerment: Stories of Women Rising Against Odds
7. Social Psychology in Everyday Life: Understanding Human Connections
8. The Essence of Motivational Speaking: Inspiring Change in Others
9. Balancing Acts: Women, Work, and the Will to Lead
10. Guiding with Grace: Raising Children with Compassion and Awareness
11. The Power of Positive Aging: Embracing Life After Fifty
12. Building Resilient Communities: Social Work in Action
13. The Ethical Educator: Principles for Teaching and Learning
14. From Insight to Impact: Social Psychology for a Better World
15. The Ethics of Empathy: A Guide to Ethical Living
16. The Science of Empowering the Self: Navigating Life's Challenges with Psychological Wisdom
17. The Mindful Conscious Leader: Meditation Techniques for Modern Management
18. Pioneering Spirit: Women's Pathways to Leadership and Empowerment
19. Feeling to Healing: The Role of Emotional Intelligence in Child Development
20. Transformative Talks and Words of Inspiration: Insights into Motivational Oratory

21. Green Ethics: A Path to Sustainable Living
22. Spiritual Integrity: Navigating Life with Moral Compassion
23. Clean Living, Clean Society: The Ethics of Cleanliness
24. Patriotic Spirits: Building a Nation on Positive Attitudes
25. Innovative Integrity & Vibrant Visions: The Ethical and Entrepreneurial Spirit of Gujarat
26. Youthful Visions, Endless Possibilities: Inspiring Ethics and Motivation in Children
27. Living Your Legacy: How to Motivate Others by Living Your Values
28. Secret of Healing Conversations: Ethical Practices in Counselling and Therapy
29. Creative Kindness: Crafting a Life of Compassion and Creativity
30. The Power of Appreciation: How Gratitude Can Transform Your Relationships
31. Bhagavad-Gita: Messages
32. Science of Art: The New Frontier of Fashion Modernism
33. Vivekananda's Virtues: A Blueprint for Modern Living
34. Empower Her: Navigating the Path to Women's Entrepreneurship
35. The Boundless Classroom: Innovations in Global Education
36. The Language of Leadership: Communicating with Authenticity and Impact
37. The Warrior's Mantra: Deciphering the Hanuman Chalisa
38. Echoes of Empathy: Transformative Stories of Social Service
39. Artful Living: Cultivating Creativity in Your Daily Routine
40. Finding Your Why: Discovering Your Passions and Charting Your Course
41. The Role of Social Media in Shaping Self-Esteem and Interpersonal Relationships among Adolescents

Contact

Dr. Minakshi Bansal
Social Activist
Ahmedabad, Gujarat, Bharat

|| LOKAHA SAMASTHAHA SUKHINO BHAVANTU ||

• 141 •